CREATING
PEACE

Transforming Ourselves
and the World

MARYA BRUNSON

LOTUS BLOSSOM BOOKS

1220 Rosecrans Street #325

San Diego, California 92106

lotusblossombooks.com

Cover and interior design: Jeff Burne Design

ISBN: 978-0-9801414-5-0

Library of Congress catalogue number pending

First printing: January 2021

PEACE

Tranquility

Harmony

Serenity

Stillness

Equanimity

This book is dedicated

to all who desire

peace on Earth

APPRECIATION

Before I offer my sincere appreciation to the selfless individuals who supported me through the writing of this book, I would like to express my gratitude for the unquenchable spirit of the human heart that, despite all odds, believes in Love and the possibility of creating peace on Earth. It was this unquenchable spirit that led me to write this book, a labor of love shared by the caring individuals who reviewed its chapters as they came to birth. Every comment, critique and suggestion they made helped the book evolve to its present state. My appreciation for their differing perspectives and candidness knows no bounds. Of these individuals, there are a few who stand out for their invaluable contributions, notably Erin Powell, who not only spent hours discussing the presentation of the book with me, but edited it as well. I am truly grateful for her insightful suggestions, as well as those made by Christina Sterling, Judy Cohan and Nancy Kael. Without their feedback and the talents of my gifted cover and interior designer, Jeff Burne, this book on Creating Peace would not have found its way to you in its present form.

My appreciation extends to those of you who care enough about peace to implement the transformative methods shared in this book. For it is your desire and ability to create a more peaceful world that will initiate the changes in perspective, attitude and action that will enable peace to become a reality on Earth.

TABLE OF CONTENTS

CHAPTER 1

THE ROAD TO PEACE

1

CHAPTER 2

CHOOSING PEACE

9

CHAPTER 3

THE EFFECT OF PROGRESS ON PEACE

19

CHAPTER 4

TAKING A QUANTUM LEAP

43

CHAPTER 5

TRANSFORMATION

51

CHAPTER 6

PRESENCE

69

CHAPTER 7

CREATING A UNIFIED WORLD

77

THE ROAD TO PEACE

We can never obtain peace in the outer world
until we make peace within ourselves.

THE DALAI LAMA

Nobody can bring you peace but yourself.

RALPH WALDO EMERSON

PEACE: An impossible dream? Or a state of being we are destined to enjoy? If we believe it's the former, our attempts will be in vain. If we understand it's the latter, we will embrace our destiny, finding ways to establish a lasting peace within ourselves and the world. Like Mahatma Gandhi, we will devote ourselves to becoming the change we wish to see in the world, not giving up until peace reigns in our hearts and evidences in our lives.

To this end, I invite you to join me on the road toward peace, searching with me for ways we can negotiate its terrain without unintentionally getting sidetracked or emotionally detained. Like traveling to any lesser known destination, we will need a road map to guide us, preferably one that has successfully guided other travelers to the peaceful state we seek. I will do my best to provide this map, sharing discoveries made by those who traveled this road before us. I believe their discoveries can help us successfully navigate the road's more challenging terrain, ultimately enabling us to experience the inner peace we long for, extending this peace to our fellow travelers here on Earth.

I realize this may seem like a lofty goal, given the current state of our world. But before we dismiss it, let's consider the countless times we have risen above our everyday expectations. Let's recall the strong feelings that impelled us to leap into unfamiliar territory, and the intuitive guidance that helped us after we got there. Let's remember how invincible and courageous we felt, how fearless and trusting we were that all would turn out well. This call to rise to a state of inner peace is no different. I am confident we can meet the challenge, because the peace we seek lives in the depth of our soul. It's simply a matter of uncovering what is already there.

One of the best ways to uncover the peace that lives within us is to become still, to quiet the thoughts, feelings and emotions keeping us too occupied to hear the whisperings of our hearts. We can find this stillness anytime, anywhere. We can find it while we stroll through gardens, parks, forests, meadows and the open countryside, or walking along the shoreline of streams, rivers, lakes or oceans. We can drop into a state of stillness while practicing yoga or meditation; or while listening to uplifting music, allowing the beauty of the music to transport us to realms beyond the stresses of our everyday lives. If none of these options are available to us, we can stop what we're doing and take a number of deep conscious breaths, paying attention to each breath as it flows gently in and out of our bodies. The method we choose is not as important as its ability to silence the barrage of thoughts, feelings and emotions keeping us in a state of unrest. At the very least, finding moments of stillness gives us a break from the stress of our busy lives and worldly concerns, something we could all use more of these days. I encourage you to give yourselves as many moments of stillness as you can. Regardless of what is going on in your lives, try to set aside a few times each day to turn to the stillness deep inside you. Persist until the chatter box in your head quiets down long enough for you to relax and experience a sense of inner calm and peace. Then go about your day, remaining as calm and peaceful as you can.

Stillness is not the only way to reduce stress and achieve a sense of well being, there are others, and they are just as powerful. Take gratitude, for instance. True appreciation for what we have does us a world of good, healing our hearts, which allows us to open to future blessings. If you question this, try a little experiment. As you wake each morning, place your hands over your heart and remember the good things and people you have in your lives: family members and friends, meaningful work, pleasant activities, or the air you breathe and the sun that warms your bodies and brightens your days. Let your hearts swell with appreciation as each blessing comes to mind. It won't take long before you will notice how powerful and effective counting your blessings can be—how doing this every day changes your lives for the better. I have found that even at the worst of times, we can always find something to be grateful for, and if we are wise, we will. For during moments of pure gratitude, every destructive thought or image, every frustrating or angry emotion is put to rest. Give gratitude a try. You've nothing to lose and everything life-affirming to gain, including some heart-felt moments of inner peace.

Forgiveness too has the power to put us on the road toward peace. Opening our hearts to genuine forgiveness frees us from the emotional pain we endure when we hold onto bitterness and resentment. It is a freedom we all desire, yet often have difficulty achieving, since our wounds can run deep and hide under layers of regret and self-condemnation. Yet, regardless of the depth of our wounds, regardless of whether they are self inflicted or inflicted by the actions of others, genuine forgiveness has the power to heal us, transforming our lives and the lives of others. Forgiving takes courage and patience. It takes empathy, compassion and the kind of love that enables us to step into the other person's shoes, to see the situation from their point of view, as well as our own. It takes a willingness to stop rationalizing and justifying our position, a willingness to let go of the hurt and anger we may feel. If we can't, if we keep rehearsing the events that caused the injury or injustice, stubbornly holding onto these events as if they were badges of honor, our injuries will continue to fester and haunt us, robbing us of the full happiness we would otherwise enjoy. I know how difficult this can be, especially when the event that haunts us involves a severe injury, the loss of someone near and dear to us, or stemmed from a traumatic or violent event. Yet forgive we must if we are ever to be at peace. For forgiving has the power to free us from the emotional pain we would otherwise carry around with us, sinking under its weight. Harboring anger, hate or vengeful emotions may seem justified when rape, murder or other heinous acts severely injure or take a life—the insanity of war included. But, if we are ever to move forward, we must find enough love in our hearts to forgive. As soon as we do, as soon as we dissolve our pain in the purifying fire of true forgiveness, the memory of the event will no longer haunt us. So let's search through our memory banks for any grievance we may be harboring, any sorrow, regret or trauma we have buried, bravely confronting it. Let's stop making excuses, stop justifying our angst, anger and resentment, stop blaming others and take responsibility for the part we are playing in our pain. Let's forgive. Let's clear the slate and move on. In other words, let's stop whatever we are doing or not doing that is keeping us from living happy contented peaceful lives.

Stillness, gratitude and forgiveness; three extremely powerful tools supporting our desire to find and maintain a state of inner peace. Do not underestimate their ability to transform your lives. They definitely have mine and they will yours as soon as you put them into practice.

CHOOSING PEACE

It isn't enough to talk about peace.
One must believe in it.
And it isn't enough to believe in it.
One must work at it.

ELEANOR ROOSEVELT

IF ASKED, most of us would say we desire to live in a peaceful world. Though, a moment later, we might add that given the current chaotic and polarized state of the world, we doubt peace will be achieved anytime soon, certainly not in our lifetime or our children's or grandchildren's lifetimes. We would most likely back up our doubts by citing the number of inhumane acts committed by our fellow humans every hour of the day, admitting how helpless we feel in the face of it all. How we believe no matter what we do, it won't significantly improve the attitudes and behaviors of the people committing these deplorable acts. Our doubts are understandable and perfectly logical if we fail to factor in the power of Love to change the minds and hearts of men. Possibly, we've not had the privilege of witnessing Love's power first hand. For if we had, we would not question its ability to awaken men to the goodness that lives deep inside them.

Our history books are filled with accounts of individuals who have born witness to the power of Love, testifying to Love's ability to wake them to the benign qualities of their higher nature. Through their writings and verbal testimonies, they have shared how Love softened their hearts, transformed their character, and altered the course of their lives. Though their accounts differ, they all convey how Love gave them the desire and strength to overcome their destructive behaviors. How it lifted them to new heights, helping them see themselves and others through a clearer, more insightful lens. How their new insights changed the course of their lives, setting them on paths they had never before considered, paths that led them toward tranquility, harmony and inner peace.

We have the same opportunity to wake to Love, allowing Love to transform us. Instead of allowing fear to be our master, instead of becoming disillusioned, disheartened and discouraged by the actions of others, we can emulate those who have accepted Love's ability to transform the minds and hearts of men. We can turn from our fears to the Love that lives at our core, allowing its purifying energy to wash through our being, freeing us from anything standing in the way of our progress and peace. We can respond to people and situations in a kind, thoughtful, generous and merciful way—even when doing this seems difficult or unpopular. We can stand up for what is right and fair, for what preserves and elevates the Earth and its people—expressing love instead of hate, calm instead of anger and peace instead of hostility, discord and strife.

Who we are, what we think, and what we do matter. Every time we allow our better nature to motivate our decisions and impel our actions we improve our lives and the lives of others—each improvement moving us and mankind a little closer to the peace our hearts tell us is possible. Sometimes doing this feels easy and natural. Goodness and kindness flows out of us without a moment's hesitation. Other times, it is hard for us to be civil, let alone thoughtful, considerate and kind. At times like these, we simply need to take a deep breath, get out of our own way, and allow the benign loving qualities of our higher nature to shine through. They are the truest part of who we are, the unblemished part that has never been submerged in a turbulent sea of negative beliefs, attitudes and emotions. All it takes is our willingness to calm and subdue this turbulent sea, silencing the negative destructive thoughts, feelings and emotions keeping us in an agitated state. When we do, the rewards are great. We are at peace and all feels right with the world.

For the sake of experimentation, I encourage you to give the following a try.

- Make an effort throughout the day to pay attention to the thoughts and images running through your minds, noticing which ones trigger negative, frustrating or hostile feelings and emotions, and which ones give you a sense of peace and well-being.

- If the thoughts running through your minds are making you feel agitated, anxious or fearful, try replacing them with positive life-affirming thoughts and images. You may have to breathe or meditate or pray before you can do this effectively.

- See how replacing your negative thoughts with positive ones helps you alter the way you are looking at situations and people. How it helps you reframe the situation or relationship in a more positive constructive way.

- Notice how reframing your viewpoint alters your feelings and emotions.

- How it helps you become calmer and less reactive, more objective and impartial.

- Realize how your new found objectivity is making you less likely to judge who is right, and who is wrong, what is right, or what is wrong.

- Then recognize how eliminating judgment is lessening your inclination to engage in arguments and disputes. Notice how the lack of these arguments and disputes improves the quality of your life.

- Be patient with yourselves. If this process is new to you it can take time, dedication and practice before it becomes natural. But in time it will, and peace will be your reward.

As indicated above, changing our habitual patterns of thought doesn't always happen overnight. Nor does becoming non-judgmental. But as we master the art, we inevitably experience a greater sense of peace and well-being. Being non-judgmental allows us to look at people and situations in a more objective, less emotional, way. Which, in the case of our relations with others, helps us find enough common ground to resolve our troubling issues. In time we come to realize that taking the high road in our dealings with others, the road paved with good will, generosity and compassion, is the most effective way to create and sustain peaceful relations.

Yes, there may be give and take. Yes, there may be compromise. And, yes, there may be times when we have to sacrifice something personally near and dear to us. But developing the ability to consider other people's points of view, allows us to make these compromises with a greater sense of ease. Something impossible to do when we are solidly entrenched in our own rigid point of view. Developing the capacity to see relationships and situations through the eyes of others, the capacity to mentally walk in their shoes, gives us a greater appreciation of their positions and requests. It helps us recognize that their needs and desires are as worthy as our own, which, in turn, helps us consider them as we negotiate the troubled waters, calming them so we can resolve the issues in question in a non-contentious, mutually beneficial and peaceful way. If we are sincere in our desire to find peace for ourselves and the world, we will do what it takes to create peace in our daily lives.

The next time a potential controversy or dispute arises in your lives, rather than becoming defensive, agitated or confrontational, pause for a few moments and breathe, continuing to breathe until you feel yourselves calming down. For when emotions are running high, and you or others are filled with hurt, anger or an uncontrollable need to be right, conflict is sure to ensue. Whereas, when you are calm, there is a much greater chance you will negotiate your differences or difficulties peaceably. Needless to say, you cannot control other's responses to your olive branch. But as you become calm, your calmness will naturally defuse the emotionally charged atmosphere, making it easier to resolve the issues at hand without rancor or, in extreme cases, bloodshed.

Taking the road that leads toward peace is a choice. A choice that becomes easier and more natural the more we make it. Eventually, we don't even have to think about it. We simply respond to people and situations from a place of Love they cannot help but feel—spreading harmony and peace one loving thought, choice and action at a time.

17

THE EFFECT OF PROGRESS ON PEACE

Peace is not merely a distant goal that we seek,
but a means by which we arrive at that goal.

MARTIN LUTHER KING JR.

EVERY DAY presents us with new opportunities to advance the cause of peace. It also presents us with new and unexpected challenges, which include learning to navigate a world that is spinning ahead at an exponential rate. A world where yesterdays beliefs, attitudes and behaviors are rapidly becoming irrelevant and outdated—where what worked a few generations ago is no longer working. What has been propelling the changes in the way our world works? A number of things to be sure, but the most obvious are the technological advances made during the last few hundred years, each requiring us to adapt to the way they are affecting our world. The changes began with the industrial advances made in England during the mid eighteenth century, spreading from England to Continental Europe, North America, Japan, and eventually the rest of the world. Advances that thrust a good percent of the world's population out of their agrarian way of life, into the industrial way of life that reigned until the mid twentieth century. Steam engines, combustion motors and factories brought people from rural areas to the cities. Cars, trains, passenger ships and airplanes began transporting them from city to city, as well as to far away places—exposing those who traveled to new cultures, foods, philosophies, religions and ways of living, some of which they incorporated into their lives. When those born in the early nineteen hundreds came into the world, the Industrial Age was in full swing. Most people living in the Western World were enjoying some, if not all, of the vast number of new products and services industry was bringing to their lives. Few considered at the time that the technology producing those products and services would soon be applied to fighting the most deadly wars in human history. It didn't occur to them that their new industrial knowhow would be applied to mechanizing the weaponry of war, allowing man's inhumanity to man to take an exponential leap from hand to hand combat and cumbersome canons to the machine guns, tanks, bombs, missiles, battleships, submarines and bomber planes used to maim and kill hundreds, even thousands, of men, women and children, in a single blow. That is, until World War II painted an inglorious picture of the horrific inhumane devastation mechanizing war had wrought.

Understandably, those who fought and died in that war felt their sacrifice was necessary and morally justified. They firmly believed they had to defend and protect those whose lives, liberties and lands were being threatened or stolen. If we were facing the same set of circumstances, we might well choose to do the same. Yet, one has to ask if maiming and murdering our fellow human beings is ever truly justified? Whether invading another's land is morally right and fair? Or if attempting to wipe out an entire tribe, race or religion is an ethical, rational or humane act?

If we sincerely desire to create peace among the peoples of Earth, it is imperative we ask ourselves these and similar questions, searching our deepest hearts and conscience for answers that reflect the spiritual values we claim to hold dear. In fact, given the technological advances that came on the heels of the Industrial Age, it is more imperative than ever that we question our proclivity toward conflict, violence and war.

We are now in a brand new age—an Information Age—where the gathering, computing, sharing and utilization of information is dominating our economy and way of life. The transformation from industry to information began when telephones, radios and phonographs found their way into our lives and homes. Motion Picture Theaters followed, captivating those who had access to them, with silent, then talking, films. Next came television, bringing the news, music, variety shows and, eventually, movies right into our living rooms. Each of these innovations affected our lives in ways we could not have anticipated, most of them in good ways, but definitely not all.

As we know, the Information Age didn't stop with the invention of telephones, radios, televisions and motion pictures. It had many new innovations in store for us. Perhaps the most impactful innovation began with the work of a team of mathematical geniuses stationed at Bletchley Park in England during the Second World War. Their mission was to protect the Allied Forces by deciphering the encrypted messages sent from the German High Command to their bombers and warships each morning. After months of failed attempts at decoding these messages, the mathematicians reluctantly decided to focus on Alan Turing's idea of developing a programmable machine that could compute data faster than the human brain. The machine, affectionately known as Colossus because of its enormous size, was not an immediate success. In fact it came close to being shuttled. However, in the end, Colossus was able to decipher the intercepted messages fed into it each morning, a feat that went a long way toward ending the war. No one, besides the mathematicians working on Colossus and the highest heads of state in England, were aware of its success until well after the close of the war. Yet, as with all progressive ideas, the idea of a programmable computing machine had found its way into the imaginative minds of other inventors, impelling them to develop similar machines, first in England, then in the United States. As with the original prototype at Bletchley Park, there were countless hurdles to overcome, yet one by one they were surmounted, and programmable computing machines became a reality. At first they were used solely by the British and United States governments, their military complexes and the research departments of large labs and universities. However, it didn't take long before these computing machines, or computers as they have come to be called, came down enough in size and price for businesses and the general public to have the use of them. Giving all who could afford a computer the ability to gather, process and share information at astonishing rates of speed.

In the 1990s search engines like Yahoo, Magellan, InfoSeek, Lycos, Excite and Google entered the scene, enabling those who lived in the developed world to access information formerly found only in books, scientific texts, journals and news publications. Using their new digital servers, researchers and citizens alike could share what they discovered with their colleagues and friends—along with their objective and subjective thoughts about it. I remember how excited my husband, a university professor, was when he first had access to an Apple computer with a Safari search engine, first in his on campus office, and then in our home. It was as if an entirely new world had opened up to him, a world he was excited to explore.

When cell phones, iPads and social media platforms, like Facebook, Instagram and Twitter, exploded onto the scene, they gave everyone who could afford a cell phone, tablet or computer round the clock opportunities to share their personal lives and opinions with the world. Openly or anonymously, they could speak their mind, influencing others for good or ill, depending on their motive or personal agenda. Before long our cellular airwaves were deluged with information—some of it accurate, informative, uplifting, helpful and entertaining, some of it inaccurate, biased, self-serving, inappropriate and down right sinister. Needless to say, being subjected to inaccurate, biased or ill intended information is not new, the human condition being what it is. Throughout history self-serving, power hungry, biased or hate filled individuals, groups and nations have been more than willing to manipulate or abandon the truth if it served their desired end. Only now the sheer volume of information flooding our devices is making it extremely difficult to separate fact from fiction or good intent from bad. Most of us simply do not have the time or inclination to do the thoughtful in-depth research and fact checking necessary to determine if the reports we are receiving are true. Which is allowing fiction to masquerade as fact, greed to masquerade as beneficial economics and hate to masquerade as a justification to inflict harm and wage war on those perceived as less than others or a threat. For peace to prevail here on Earth, it is not only vital that we expose these masquerades, but equally vital that we obliterate their desired effect by refusing to react emotionally to the negative information flooding our devices, newspapers and television screens—diligently checking reports out before we form an opinion or offer a response. Even when distressing information turns out to be true, we are well served to not become reactive or aggressive in our response. But rather, to turn to and listen to the voice of our conscience for the most conscientious, peace preserving, response. Doing this consistently to thwart the plans of those who gain advantage by agitating society, pushing it toward conflict and war.

Not surprisingly, there are those who are using social media to intentionally sew the seeds of unrest. Motivated by a combination of fear, prejudice, hate, greed and insecurity, they are plying the digital airwaves with well-crafted slanderous posts about groups or individuals who threaten their beliefs, ambitions and way of life. Social media platforms have simply given them a bully pulpit from which to defame the lives of others, in order to gain their desired ends. It has also given them a way to lure the naive and unsuspecting to their philosophy and points of view, stirring them into a floury of reactive responses. Those who are committed to peace have an opportunity to be a counterbalancing force to this destructive divisive behavior, making use of social media to spread the truth, as well as the necessity for love, compassion, mercy, goodness and forgiveness. Yes, forgiveness. I understand forgiving those who are telling lies and slandering us or others is not easy. But, without forgiveness there can be no peace. And peace, after all, is what we are aiming for, our own peace, as well as peace for the rest of mankind. So in the interest of creating peace, let's make it a habit to forgive those who have become so detached from their conscience they have no qualms about lying or vilifying us or others. We can set the record straight, but only if we do this in a way that doesn't rob us of our integrity and inner sense of peace. Punishment or retaliation for others' lies and distortions cannot be our motive. The law of karma will do a much better job of setting those of little conscience straight—bringing them face to face with their immoral deeds, forcing them at some point to feel the brunt of those very deeds. Realizing this helps us rise above our hurt or need to aggressively respond. Understanding that those who are without conscience will suffer from the cut of their own sword, not as punishment, but as a way to awaken them to the higher values and behaviors of their soul. So, let's not waste our energy suffering from the immoral acts of others. In time, they will see the error of their ways. In the meantime, be their example. Stand with and for Love. Be merciful and forgiving to the innocent and guilty alike.

Let us also watch our words. For the words we use have the power to influence those receiving them. They can unite or divide, soothe or agitate, promote peace or incite confusion, enmity, conflict and war. If we truly want to create a peaceful society, we must do our best to choose our words carefully, using only those that are truthful and beneficial to those who receive them. In addition, we would do well to thoughtfully consider other people's words, responding in ways that contribute to their welfare, as well as our own. Doing our best to overcome any inclination to become self-righteous and judgmental, angrily championing a group, cause or policy we know little or nothing about. In this day of misleading information, divisiveness and populist leanings, it is more important than ever for us to respond to people and events with calmness, clarity, objectivity and, grace, regardless of the temptation to do otherwise. This is especially true when we consider how the following technical advances are challenging our prospects for peace.

Unbeknownst to us, the algorithms employed by high tech search engines gave a great number of companies access to our personal information, such as our financial status, likes, dislikes, opinions, colleagues, friends, ethnicities, religious preferences and political leanings. The nature of business being what it is, some of these companies chose to add to their revenue stream by selling this information—without our knowledge or consent. This, in turn, has allowed their buyers to use this information to influence us, again without our knowledge or consent. The information purchased by ad agencies and marketing firms to bring products to our attention is not new. Marketers have found ways to sell us products since the sale of goods began. However, the information purchased by other groups and organizations has not been as obvious or above board. Instead, it has been surreptitiously used to sway us toward the buyers religious, economic or political agendas. When we add that hackers have been hired by political organizations and governments to plant false or misleading information on social media sites to sway or confuse us, the picture begins to look even more complex and grim. Most troubling and disruptive, for example, was Russia's use of social media platforms to influence the outcome of the 2016 presidential election in the United States and the United Kingdom's Brexit vote to leave the European Union. Fortunately, people of conscience courageously made us aware of these practices, hoping to reign them in. Yet, as we have discovered, reigning them in is not as simple as we would like, even when some social media companies are willing to devote time and expertise to policing their sites, removing a number of the hacker's false or misleading posts. Thereby, it is vital we do our part, checking out the information we receive through social media, before jumping to conclusions, allowing ourselves to become incensed or outraged over the depiction of events that may be false or misleading. False or not, outrage is never the best response, certainly not one that creates or supports peace, much as we might wish that it were.

As with all things in life, the use of our ever advancing technology is a matter of conscience. We can use it to improve, elevate and ease our lives and the lives of others. Or we can use it to promote private, group or national agendas—warping the information we post to appeal to men's fears, intentionally breeding confusion and chaos to keep people at odds with each other. If peace is our goal, it is imperative we follow the dictates of our conscience, allowing it to guide us in our use of social media, as well as all the other areas of our lives. To do this effectively, we need to quiet ourselves enough to actually hear the voice of our conscience, silencing the jumble of thoughts, feelings and emotions raging inside us. Then, upon hearing, we must be willing to follow its sage advice, at all times and in all ways. Using the information tools at our disposal to uplift the spirit of those who receive our messages, spreading love for humanity and hope and faith for a brighter future. If we are scientists or researchers, we can use these tools to share our research with other scientists and researchers in order to advance the human condition—like finding cures and treatments for diseases, such as the Corona Virus currently threatening lives throughout the world. We can use them to help us brainstorm and implement solutions to the economic disparities causing so much inequity and suffering; or to encourage people to prioritize equality, justice, the climate crisis and peace between peoples and nations.

It is hard to believe our conscience would impel us to use our technological expertise to create sophisticated weaponry that, if put into the wrong hands, could destroy mankind in a matter of minutes. Or that it would have us entrust the use of this sophisticated weaponry solely to our military commanders and heads of state. Making it all the more imperative that we consider the history and character of those we choose to govern our townships, cities and nations, selecting only those who have proven their willingness to follow the high moral and spiritual values of their conscience.

Many people sincerely believe that possessing sophisticated high tech weapons is a deterrent to war, that being able to access them at a moments notice is keeping their families, homes and nations safe. Yet, are they? Are not people being injured and killed by the use of modern weapons every hour of every day? History tells us, if weapons exist, someone somewhere can, and most likely will, find a way use them. If we take into account all the nuclear missiles and bombs stockpiled around the world, the possibility of governments or military leaders launching one or more of them is far from comforting. One has to question whether these high tech weapons can actually produce the peace we claim we desire. Logic would say it is highly unlikely, as weapons developed to destroy life have nothing in common with that which preserves and protects life. To quote Albert Einstein: "Peace cannot be kept by force, it can only be achieved by understanding." Yet here we are, sitting on a powder keg of our own making, mankind's survival dependent on the restraint of a handful of leaders who have the power to push a button or order a strike that could plunge the world into a nuclear nightmare. It is ever more incumbent upon us to make sure those who have this awesome power are intelligent, high-minded, thoughtful, rational, moral human beings, practiced in the art of restraint. Leaders with a sincere desire to not only improve the lives of those who live in their nations, but who have the desire and ability to implement policies that are capable of producing peaceful relations between people and nations throughout the world.

In truth, we are all well served when we listen to and follow the divine whispers of our conscience—even when doing this is challenging—when the world is so noisy and distracting it is hard for us to hear, let alone respond, to the superior guidance our conscience offers. And, when we do hear, having the willingness to put our personal desires and fears aside long enough to follow its dictates. There are times when doing this is relatively easy. Other times when it requires faith, trust and a fair amount of courage to comply—abilities in short supply if we are not used to experiencing them. If we are honest, most of us have to admit there have been times in our lives when we have ignored the sage advise of our conscience. Like those who commit the acts we deplore, we have behaved in a manner unbefitting our better nature. Moments when we have allowed ourselves to see people as enemies across a divide, regardless of the nature of those enemies or the breadth of that divide. Our primitive instincts have kicked in, enticing us to descend to a level far beneath the dignity of our true nature. We'd like to think of ourselves as high-minded moral human beings, ready to fight the good fight for what we believe is right. Yet, as Gandhi and other wise individuals have aptly pointed out, fighting against something usually tends to inflame it, rather than reducing it to provide the harmonious effect our deepest hearts intend. Whereas consciously tapping into and habitually reflecting the qualities and behaviors of our higher nature, decreases our impulse to resort to anger, conflict or force. As more of us are able to live in accord with the high standard our conscience reflects, the evils within our society will be exposed and corrected without having to sacrifice the lives of the innocent to achieve the peace we desire.

Until we have evolved, until the primitive beliefs behind our divisive behaviors have been uncovered and annihilated, they will continue to fester, bursting into flame when we least expect it. Winning a battle or war might feel satisfying in the short run, but it doesn't rid either side of the polarizing beliefs, attitudes, grievances and protectionism that led them to war against each other in the first place. One has to ask if it is rational to believe that killing people is justified if our cause is just? Or that all will be well when we win? This argument is not only illogical and immoral, but hard to support when both sides truly believe their cause is just. We must agree with Einstein and Gandhi, who understood that fighting anything or anyone is not a sound recipe for peace. On the contrary, it adds fuel to the fire, inflaming minds and hearts on both sides, blinding them to the great benefits love and cooperation can bring. Would it not be more fruitful to find peaceful ways to bridge the divides that exist between ourselves and others; more practical to create policies and alliances that benefit both? Regardless of our good intentions, or the moral, egalitarian, democratic ideals we are willing to fight and die for, would we not be better served to follow the higher, peace preserving, ideals that foster the building of a cooperative harmoniously interactive society? Would it not be more productive and less costly to reach an olive branch out to those who appear to be on the other side of the divide? All the military might in the world cannot deliver an honorable lasting peace. For the wounds of war not only maim and kill our bodies, they fester in our minds and hearts, standing in the way of our achieving the lasting peace we would otherwise enjoy. Given this outcome, would it not be wiser to seek peaceful solutions to our issues and differences? Would not diplomacy and compromise be more likely to produce a more positive end result—helping us create a more cooperative, mutually beneficial, harmonious and peaceful society in which all can not only survive, but thrive?

Scientists are making discoveries every day that have the potential to make life easier, healthier and more rewarding for the peoples of Earth. All it takes is our willingness to adopt the discoveries that have the greatest potential for good. It also takes heeding their warnings—especially about the destructive impact our past and present behaviors are having on Earth's environment. For years environmental scientists have been warning us that our mining and use of fossil fuels, the clear cutting of rainforests and our large consumption of meat is having a destructive impact on Earth's atmosphere and ecosystems. That if we don't change our ways, we could be the next species to become extinct. Many have heeded their warnings, supporting the development and use of alternate sources of energy and more healthful ways to produce and preserve the foods and products they consume. Acutely aware that the degradation and repair of the planet's environment will fall squarely on their shoulders, the young have become some of Earth's fiercest environmental advocates, doing their best to encourage their elders to take positive action before the rapid glacier melts, massive floods, severe droughts, fires and rising oceans devastate more of Earth's habitable areas. Along with our youth, scientists and environmentalists have vociferously pointed out that, in addition to our conflicts and wars, the warming of Earth's atmosphere is the biggest contributor to the mass migrations we have been witnessing. When lands are no longer able to sustain those who live on them, the people living in those lands have no choice but to migrate to more hospitable areas. Understanding the plight of those fleeing from parched barren lands, as well as from conflicts and wars, the kind hearted have welcomed migrating families into their communities, integrating them into their work force and schools. However, the fearful have not been as welcoming, concerned their way of life will be adversely affected by the growing population and the influence of other cultures. The clash between those extolling compassion and inclusion and those trumpeting exclusion and isolation has led to heated arguments and an ever growing divide. Certainly, not to the peace many of those same people claim they desire.

It would appear that resistance to change is a malady we all share. To some degree, we have a tendency to hold onto what is familiar, our latent fear of the unknown holding us back from fully embracing what Life has to offer. Though no one can accurately predict what will come around the next corner, we all know it is bound to bring change. As change is an integral part of life. Babies don't remain babies. They grow into toddlers, children, teenagers and adults. So it is with all the chapters of our lives. We can try to resist, clinging tenaciously to the life we know. But, with or without our consent, Life will have its way with us, pulling us into a future that is unlike our past. All our resistance will have been in vain. So, rather than clinging to life as we know it, we might as well surrender to the inevitable progressions Life is bringing, anticipating the best, the way we do when we're planning to travel to a part of the world we've not seen, but have heard is amazing. When we travel, we bring what we need, leaving the rest behind. It is the same with the progressions of Life. We need to bring the best of us along, leaving the rest behind, especially the beliefs, habits and emotional baggage no longer serving us. Not just the obvious beliefs and habits we've accumulated during our lifetime, but the hereditary inclinations and habits hiding under layers of unconscious acceptance: like the primitive cellular imprints buried in the collective psyche and our personal DNA, including the fight or flight fear response etched during our ancestor's hunter/gatherer days. Considering how much we have evolved since then, it's clearly past time to toss these primitive responses into the ash heap of history. They served another time, a way of life long gone, certainly not the evolutionary stage we currently live in, let alone the more progressive one looming on the horizon. So instead of responding to the primitive fear lurking in the collective psyche and the cells of our DNA, let's do all we can to override these outmoded influences, changing the way we see and respond to the world and its people. Instead of seeing enemies lurking around every corner and border, let's choose to see those we don't know as potential friends, with as much to give and teach us as we have to give and teach them. Let's embrace every day with a sense of exuberance and positive expectation, eager to grow, to approach every situation, good or bad, as an opportunity to expand our awareness and find ways to bring the peoples of Earth into one accord.

This is the way of the new age. A way not bound by the ancient codes that belonged to our long dead ancestors. It is a way that proceeds from an altitude of positivity, trust and a willingness to accept the new as it unfolds—a way that allows us to plant our feet firmly on the road toward peace.

TAKING A QUANTUM LEAP

Everything changes
Nothing remains without change . . .

BUDDHA

Step out of the circle of time and into the circle of love.

RUMI

DURING MAN'S TENURE here on Earth, there have been times when an unexpected shift in man's consciousness imposed a major evolutionary change. Now is one of those times. A time when we are undergoing a shift as life-altering as the one that catapulted our ancestors out of their two-dimensional perception of life into the three-dimensional perception we have experienced since the shift occurred. Like our ancestors, we can attempt to hang back in an outworn state, believing in myths and hoping to live in ways we are used to, or we can cross into the more expansive state looming on the horizon, enjoying the enormous benefits its broader scope has to offer.

Think about the wondrous new vistas of thought, exploration and discovery our ancestors experienced when they finally let go of their limited two-dimensional perception of life. Then imagine what life will be like when we let go of the limitations of our current perception, adopting the more expansive view looming on the horizon. Imagine how our lives will change when we become more aware of the underlying interconnectedness that bonds us with the rest of humanity. How our awareness of this bond will impact the way we interact with our fellow human beings. How it will impel us to be more caring, compassionate, fair, just and respectful, championing everyone's right to life, liberty and the pursuit of health and happiness. Imagine how our new found awareness will deepen our sense of love, and how this deeper sense of love will become the overriding force in our lives, encouraging us to create the kind of relationships and alliances that will pave the way for a lasting global peace.

As this evolutionary shift is already imposing itself upon the consciousness of mankind, we can do more than imagine. We can cooperate, preparing ourselves for this evolutionary shift by devoting quality time each day to expanding and clarifying our perception of life. We can silence the influence of the world's antiquated beliefs by meditating and praying, filling our hearts with gratitude and cleansing them with forgiveness. We can cultivate our intuitive ear, the ear that is always tuned to the voice of our conscience, the keen inner ear that hears and is devoted to Truth and Love, welcoming their guidance and protection, their merciful view of humankind. We can celebrate every insight, ah ha moment, epiphany and revelation that dawns on us, allowing each to transform us from the persons we believe ourselves to be, to the more conscious insightful caring beings we truly are.

Should we not feel quite ready to make this commitment, choosing to remain in the familiar constructs of our current paradigm, we will soon discover these constructs don't work well in today's interactive global society. We will realize they are too insular, too limited, too intolerant and intransigent to effectively navigate the world's current terrain. We will realize we are swimming against the tide, that our attempts to cling to outmoded ways are being met with an unrelenting counterforce. That something beyond our control is forcing us to shift into more conscious states of being, whether we feel ready to or not. We can fight this shift with every fiber of our being, lashing out against integration and unification, but in the end we will realize we are not strong enough to hold back Life's progression, and it is pointless for us to try. Life will thrust us forward, with or without our consent, utilizing circumstance after circumstance to convince us to yield to the higher ideals and deeper sense of Love that belongs to the age of enlightenment we are entering. Experiencing this deeper, more inclusive, sense of Life and Love is our destiny— mankind's destiny. As distant and unrealistic as this destiny may seem at the moment, mankind will inevitably see the wisdom of forming national and global policies and alliances that can provide every man, woman and child on Earth an opportunity to live well.

Granted, it may take time for this deeper awareness to take root in the collective consciousness, but at some point it will not only take root, it will grow and mature until unity and peace become a reality. When the majority of humans finally wake to the higher mode of life that is their destiny, all the hatred, fear, greed and lust for power that have plagued man's existence, will cease. Love will take their place as the motivating force behind the majority of men's choices and actions. How long this will take, no one knows for sure. It could take fifty years or a thousand. But, at some point the humans populating the Earth will emulate their two-dimensional ancestors, taking a quantum leap into a more expansive enlightened state of being.

The good news is, we don't have to wait for the majority of humans to take this leap before we do. We can choose to leap now, consciously letting go of our antiquated notions, replacing them with the more inclusive understanding of life that is true to the dimension reeling us in. It doesn't matter if we accomplish this in small incremental barely noticeable transitions, in sudden bursts of insight and inspiration, or a combination of both. Whenever and however insights dawn on us, they will give us a clearer understanding of life and the connective tissue that unites all the expressions of Life into a cohesive whole. When Life is understood from this inclusive perspective, "Do unto others as we would have them do unto us," takes on an entirely new level of meaning—not only motivating us to do no harm, but inspiring us to build healthy, mutually beneficial, relationships with our fellow human beings and the natural world. So, let's not wait for the rest of mankind to get onboard. Let's be brave and ride the transformational wave into the new age of enlightenment that is our destiny. Let's willingly shift through paradigm after paradigm until we are ready to take a quantum leap into the higher dimensional understanding and experience of life, where harmony and peace are the norm.

TRANSFORMATION

*Our progress Spiritward is in proportion
to the illumination which enables us to behold
more and more of Reality.*

JOEL GOLDSMITH
The Infinite Way

PEACE IS A STATE OF MIND, a state of the heart, a state of consciousness. A state we will experience as soon as we transform into the more enlightened selfless beings we are intended to be. Everything good and holy within us is supporting this transformation. Encouraging us to surrender to the purifying power of Truth sweeping through our consciousness, cleansing us of anything stunting our growth or stagnating the forward trajectory of our lives. Urging us to exchange our shadow selves for the higher versions of ourselves we've glimpsed, but rarely been able to sustain. Maintaining this ideal may have been challenging while we were caught in the restrictiveness of old paradigms, but times have changed. The millennium we are living in is not only geared to support our transformation, it is forcing us to make it. Rattling our cage if we resist or revert to the outworn self-absorbed sense of ourselves we have carried around for far too long. The selfless soul that lives deep inside us wants us to be free of our ego-selves. It wants us to stop carrying them around, like millstones, weighing us down, preventing us from transforming into the selfless enlightened beings we are intended to be. Our selfless soul has been trying to get our attention, knocking on the door of our everyday consciousness, devising ways to get us to recognize the benign qualities of our true nature. It is knocking right now, softly at first, bringing us gentle reminders of who we are and how we are intended to live. If we fail to notice its gentle knocks, or notice, but choose to ignore them, they will amp up their volume, knocking louder and more forcefully until they break down the walls of our resistance, insisting we exchange our ego-selves for the selfless selves that define our true nature.

It goes without saying, that responding when our soul knocks softly, is wise. For it spares us years of crisis, pain and suffering. Pain that may seem unbearable or break our mortal hearts when we, or those we care about, are caught in its clutches. At times like these, it is comforting to realize that suffering and pain disappear when we no longer need them as prods to get our attention. In the meantime, it is helpful to think about crisis as a message from our soul, a clarion call imploring us to exchange the predilections and habits of our ego-selves for the selfless benign qualities and behaviors of our higher nature. At the height of our suffering we may pray for these clarion calls to stop, but our soul has no intention of giving up on us. It will keep calling, insisting that we transform. We all have dramatic tales we can tell of times in our lives when our soul has shaken up our lives, forcing us to turn within for direction and counsel. I have definitely had my share.

My first husband fought in the Korean war years before I met him. Like many veterans he returned from the war with a number of deep emotional scars, scars he covered up so well few were aware of their existence. Post traumatic stress was unknown at the time, or at least not diagnosed and treated as it is today, so veterans were left on their own to deal with their trauma and pain. To anyone observing, me included, it appeared that my charming, talented, larger than life, husband had successfully dealt with the wounds he carried home from the war. But, the fact is, he had not. By the time the event took place I'm about to relate, his seemingly casual social drinking had escalated to full blown alcoholism, repeatedly plunging our family into dire and traumatic situations. At one point things got so bad I had to ask my mother to fly to Manhattan, and take our children back with her to California. Shortly after they departed, during one of our darkest hours, Alcoholics Anonymous came to our rescue, giving me hope for a bright new future. Unfortunately, that hope proved to be short lived, creating a number of situations that prompted us to return to California. On our way, my husband's drinking escalated, leaving us both in an untenable situation, as I did not drive at the time. After a series of close calls and scary moments I insisted we stop at an interstate truck stop so he could get some coffee and food, and, hopefully sober up enough to drive. I remember getting out of the car to stretch my legs and take our dogs for a walk on the large open field behind the truck stop, praying for an answer to our dilemma. My aching motherly heart was desperate to make it home safely to our children. After communing with God and my soul for what seemed a very long time, I suddenly felt an impulse to return with our dogs to the car. Within minutes of our return, my husband sauntered up with a young couple in tow. He announced they were hitchhiking to San Francisco and were hoping they could hitch a ride with us. Though there was little room for two extra people in our car, something deep inside told me to consider it. "Do you drive?" I asked. "We do," the young man replied, clearly understanding my husband was in no shape to drive. "But I don't have my drivers license with me. She does though." "Would you be willing to drive?" I asked her. "If you would, you can travel to Los Angeles with us, taking a bus from there to San Francisco." As it turns out, she was more than willing, said she loved to drive and was thrilled they'd be able to make it safely to San Francisco in time for an event they needed to attend. I honestly can't recall what the event was, perhaps a friend's wedding. But I do recall how deeply grateful I was that my prayerful surrender had unearthed a perfect and timely solution. One that not only blessed my husband and me, but the young couple as well. Soul may have plunged me into that crisis, and many before it, to get my attention, but I knew deep down that it was my willingness to get my fearful sense of self out of the way, that supplied the solution. It may have taken a series of these strong messages from my soul before I was willing to consistently exchange the desires of my human heart for the desires of my soul, but over the years I have come to trust my soul knows best. I am sure many of you have come to trust that yours does as well. Sadly, my husband was never able to heal the deep emotional wounds he received in the war, so though we did safely reach California and our children, in the end, he did not survive. Much as we would wish it otherwise, not everyone is ready to forgive the sins they've committed against their soul, nor let go of the trauma and pain torturing them—despite the depth and sincerity of our love and prayers.

On a grander scale, it has taken ages for mankind to recognize the promise embedded in its collective soul, but here we are, with an unprecedented opportunity to not only recognize this promise, but to so fully respond, we become living examples of the happier, healthier, more productive, beings we are intended to be. Transforming gives us this opportunity to not only bless ourselves, but all mankind. As we are an integral part of the collective we call mankind, contributing to the state of the collective consciousness, raising or lowering it accordingly. Thereby, as we transform into higher versions of ourselves, our elevated state of consciousness impacts the rest of mankind, making it easier for others to transform. For example, as we become more aware of our higher intelligence, more aware of our ability to know what our intellect does not know, we are clearing a pathway for others to tap into their own higher intelligence, their own intuitive wisdom and ability to download creative ideas never before known to man. Tapping into our intuitive wisdom enables us to be conduits for new scientific, philosophical, spiritual and creative breakthroughs, enabling us to forge new pathways in the areas of our special interest. Everyone has the innate ability to download information from their higher intelligence. Signs of it can be seen everywhere: people receiving and responding to their intuition, their sixth sense, their hunches and ah ha moments.

Many years ago during one of the actress chapters of my life, I was working at a studio in Hollywood, shooting an episode of Assignment Underwater. During a scene toward the end of the shoot, my role as an underwater photographer required me to dive into a large tank of water that was part of the scenic designer's underwater grotto. No one thought twice about me making this dive, as I knew how to swim and the tank was not much deeper than a swimming pool. However, needing to stay out of the camera's view of the scene still in progress, I had dived to the bottom of the pitch dark tank, assuming it would take me longer to return to the surface. After touching bottom, I instinctively turned upward, unintentionally heading up inside the hollow of the plaster rock submerged in the tank—my scuba gear catching on the outside of the plaster rock. I remember struggling to free the tank from the rock, wondering if I wasn't able to, if the tank actually contained air for me to breathe. Just as I was starting to panic, one of the lead actors, sensing I was in trouble, dove into the tank and dislodged my scuba gear from the rock—saving me from drowning in a ten foot tank. Intuition? Sixth sense? Whichever it was, he had sensed I was in trouble and followed his hunch. I will ever be grateful for his intuitive response.

This special type of intelligence has been impressing itself upon humans since HomoSapiens first appeared on Earth. In every age it has guided and directed them, protecting them whenever they were paying attention. This inner guide is always at work, helping us navigate our way through life. When things go awry, it shows us how to put them right. When we find ourselves in the midst of physical or emotional storms, it directs us toward the eye of the storm, urging us to stay in the safety of the eye until the storm blows over. I have no doubt you have benefited from its wise counsel. I know I have many times.

I recall a time when I was picnicking in a park with my children and an older friend, when a gang of rough looking young men came upon us, taunting and harassing us. As one of them picked up an apple from our picnic blanket, tossing it into the air, the leader of the gang marched up to me and, with a sinister sneer on his face, announced that he and his gang could do anything they wanted to us. Instead of becoming fearful or aggressively protective, I remember standing very still, not making a sound or moving a muscle as I searched within myself for the right way to handle the situation. "See who he really is," I kept hearing my inner voice say. Obeying, I looked through the young man's eyes, attempting to connect with his soul. Then, with a sense of authority that came from the depth of my own soul, I said: "No, you can't, because the principle inside you won't let you." He stood there in shock for a moment, not believing his ears. A minute later he spun around and signaled to his gang, directing them to follow him to another part of the park—which they did, none of them questioning why or disputing his authority.

Connecting with the divinity of who he was had awakened that insight in him, if only for a moment, allowing the situation to resolve without incident. On other occasions as well, I have found that connecting with the divine essence of myself and others has defused the electrical charge in the atmosphere, allowing challenging situations to resolve in a non-confrontational way. Each has given me an opportunity to become the change I wanted to see in others. If I wanted or needed someone to hold to a higher standard, I had to uphold that standard first. If I wanted someone to be more just and fair, I had to make sure I was being just and fair, rather than pushing my own agenda or point of view. If someone was seeing things from a skewed, prejudiced or selfish point of view, I had to make sure my ego-self was out of the way, that it was not tempting me to become self righteous, or demand others see things the way I would wish, but rather doing what I had done in the park that day, connecting with the sinlessness of their soul and my own. A sense of soul that doesn't rush to judgment, anger or resentment, but is able to uphold a deeper divine justice, allowing that justice to evidence itself without my ego's interference.

Connecting with the divinity that dwells within us and others is a powerfully effective form of prayer. A form that dissolves the separateness we normally feel between ourselves and others or between ourselves and the Divine Force we call God. I have found that aligning with this Divine Force, as well as the essence of my higher self and the higher self of others, is more effective than prayers of supplication, especially prayers outlining what I want or think is best. Not that prayers for healing are not worthy, they are, but as they start from the premise that someone or something is unwell, they unintentionally reinforce that unwell state in our consciousness. Whereas, recognizing and acknowledging the intrinsic wholeness that exists beneath the appearance of illness, injury or unhealthy relationships, activates that sense of wholeness, making it more available and demonstrable. Once you experience the power of this type of exalted prayer, understanding first hand how transformative and healing it is, I'm sure you too will be led to pray in this special way.

Try a little experiment.

- Find a place where you will be undisturbed.

- Turn within. Quiet your mind and move into your heart. Move from your heart to the quiet sanctuary of your soul.

- Surrender to the Divine Force that generates, governs and regulates the universe. You can think of this Force as God if this seems warmer to you.

- Open yourselves to its healing power, inviting this healing power to flow through the entirety of your consciousness and the pores of your body.

- Invite this Divine Force to dissolve anything obvious or hidden that may be crippling or condemning you or others—any thought, memory, resentment, grievance, judgment or sacrifice.

- Accept that you and others can be free of these crippling interlopers.

- Surrender your attachment to each crippler as it surfaces, letting it go.

- Surrender your sorrows or sense of guilt. Accept that you can be free enough of them to transform.

- Trust that the divinity within you and others knows how to resolve differences amicably, justly and peaceably. That it is enlightening you right now, correcting whatever misconceptions you are laboring under.

- Sit in this transformative, error correcting, state for as long as you can.

- Bask in the resolutions you know are at hand. Trust and accept that your difficulties are being resolved right now. Trust until all the conflicting thoughts and emotions inside you dissolve, and a sense of comfort and peace returns.

- Give thanks to the Divine Force that is God and your soul for your transformation and renewed sense of peace.

The good news is: the Omnipotent, Omniscient, Omnipresent Force we call God is ever revealing and reinforcing Truth within consciousness—not your truth or my truth, but Truth itself. All it takes is going deep enough within ourselves to become aware of this Truth, allowing it to expose the erroneous conceptions masquerading in its name.

As you and I become more and more conscious of Truth, all the untruths and misconceptions we are laboring under, begin to fall away, allowing us to recognize and transform into the enlightened, principled, loving versions of ourselves our deepest hearts know we are. This transformation doesn't usually happen overnight, though it can. Either way, and to whatever degree, our heightened awareness changes our lives and the lives of others for the better. There are countless testimonials to this phenomena. Deepak Chopra, in his book, "Peace is the Way" sites a few, including the carefully controlled study done by members of the Transcendental Meditation community between June 7 and July 30, 1993. Using police reports to verify the beneficial effects of group meditation, a specific number of TM meditators joined together for two week periods in Washington DC to demonstrate the transformative effect of group meditation on violent crime. As they knew it would, violent crime significantly decreased during the time of their meditation, despite the blistering heat and the downturn in the economy. Thus proving beyond the shadow of a doubt that being in a deep state of meditative consciousness not only benefits the meditator, but has a beneficial impact on the behavior of others as well—in this instance, significantly reducing the violent or nefarious tendencies of those living in Washington D.C. If group meditation can alter the violent tendencies of those living in a major city, it can certainly do the same in all cities, towns and villages in the world. Therefore, along with all the practical things we can do to make this world a better place, it's good to know that dropping into a state of meditative stillness not only improves our lives, but positively affects the state of the collective consciousness, helping humans everywhere discover the benign qualities that live at their core. The acceptance and expression of those qualities paving the way for peace to become a reality within themselves and the collective community of man.

PRESENCE

The only thing that's real in any universe [is] that brilliant fire of Love that burns to the exclusion of everything else.

—— RICHARD BACH ——

Know that you are a miracle and that you have a unique place in the cosmic plan. You are here to be the presence of love. You are here to be the presence of joy. You are here to be the presence of peace.

—— DEEPAK CHOPRA ——

OUR ABILITY TO LIVE AT PEACE with one another is inextricably linked to the state of our conscious awareness, especially our awareness of Love—the unconditional, forgiving, merciful, compassionate and embracive Love that spills into the atmosphere, filling everything it touches with an indescribable sense of warmth, comfort and peace. The kind of love that comes from the depth and purity of our hearts, endowing us with grace as it nourishes us and the world around us.

We can feel it flowing freely from the presence of illumined masters and others of high consciousness. Yet, we can also feel it in a tender touch, the purity of nature and the innocence of babies and gentle animals. It is a presence we are all meant to experience—a presence the majority of us must experience for peace to become a reality here on Earth.

In addition to tapping into the transformative power of Truth, we would do well to steep ourselves in the all-encompassing presence of Love—cultivating this presence each and every day.

- We can begin by acknowledging the reality of divine Love, accepting it is available to us and all.

- We can desire to understand and express this Love, opening ourselves to Love's powerful transformative presence, inviting it to permeate the entirety of our being, dislodging anything dark or fearful that might be hiding in the crevices of our psyche or subconscious.

- We can spend time each day immersing ourselves in this special kind of Love, inviting it to dissolve our grief and regrets, our loneliness and feelings of rejection.

- We can embrace the new found sense of peace Love is bringing to our lives, holding onto this peace as we move through our days.

- We can strive to be like Love, to be a reflection of Love here on Earth, exuding its tranquility, harmony and peace, regardless of circumstances.

- We can trust that this same tranquility, harmony and peace lives deep inside the heart and soul of every man, woman and child on Earth, and that each is capable of recognizing and experiencing it—capable of experiencing the presence of Love, the presence of harmony, the presence of peace.

We may not experience the fullness of Love's presence right away. But the more we consecrate ourselves to Love, the more we open ourselves to its healing transformative presence, steeping ourselves in the comfort of its peace, the more we will carry this comforting peace into our lives. Regardless of the activities or people we are engaged with, there will be a part of us that is so present with Love, we will see all that is going on through Love's eyes. Without knowing how it happened, we will have become the observer, as well as the engaged participator in the happenings of our lives. This witnessing part of us is detached from the trials and tribulations that come into our lives and the lives of others; not detached in a cold-hearted uncaring way, but in a deeply conscious loving angelic way that helps us handle each trial with grace. Like a mother kissing the bruised knee of her child to make it feel better, our angelic witnessing presence will be kissing the bruised knees of our lives, helping our lives heal and transform in ways the mortal sense of us could not have imagined.

There will come a time when we are hyperaware of Love's presence, aware that Love is always with us, ready to meet our needs, put balm on our wounds, and a lightness of spirit in our hearts. That by elevating our minds, expanding our hearts and resurrecting our souls it is helping us live in accord with the laws and unifying principles regulating and governing the universe—laws and principles that establish our true relationship with every form of life. There will come a time when we will see through the false structures upon which mortal life is built, replacing them with more inclusive, egalitarian, just structures that support the needs of all. A time when we will truly be a walking breathing presence of Love. The wise witnessing presence of us knows this, trusts this and foresees a time when we and the collective consciousness of mankind will be so filled with Love, peace will prevail on Earth.

So, instead of cringing at the horrific deeds being done by our fellow humans, succumbing to despair over the hopelessly divided conditions of our nations and society—instead of rising up in righteous indignation or falling to the level of those we disparage by resorting to physical violence to right the wrongs we perceive in society, let's fill ourselves with the healing balm of Love, letting Love transform our hearts and guide our actions, showing us the most effective ways to foster the understanding and cooperation that will bring peace to our troubled world.

As mentioned above, peace is a state of mind, a state of the heart, a state of consciousness—a state we naturally enjoy when we are fully immersed in the presence of Love. Others can feel the love exuding from us. When it's strong it can help them tap into the love that lives in the depth of their own hearts and souls, awakening them to this pure sense of Love in the process. It is said: fear begets fear and violence begets violence. But you will find that Love is stronger than all the fear and violence men can conjure—strong enough to wipe out all the evils warping the consciousness and lives of men.

Being immersed in the presence of the now is creative and enlivening. Being immersed in the presence of Truth is transformative and healing. Being immersed in the presence of Love is purifying and transcendent, endowing us with a holiness and grace that elevates our being as nothing else can. We become magnanimous, merciful, generous, compassionate and forgiving, instinctively mothering the earth and all of its people. Nothing holds a candle to Love for meeting our needs, especially our need to live in a peaceful world. Let us set our sights high and aim to reflect Love. Let's spend quality time each day turning within to the Love that lives deep inside us, immersing ourselves in its comforting peaceful presence, carrying this presence with us wherever we go. Let's hold onto the transcendent spirit of Love—trusting it can, and ultimately will, free us and all who are caught in the clutches of fear, and the demoralizing hatred, envy, jealousy, greed and lust for power, resulting from fear. Let's aim to be Love's presence here on Earth. We can. It's simply a matter of choice.

7

CREATING A UNIFIED WORLD

We are already one. But we imagine we are not.
And what we have to recover is our original unity.
What we have to be is what we are.

THOMAS MERTON

So powerful is the light of unity
that it can illuminate the whole earth.

BUDDHA

LOVE IS THE GLUE that binds humanity into a coherent, cohesive, interdependent whole—a united community of souls linked together at the deepest levels of their being. Despite appearances to the contrary, it is a link that has never been broken. It exists to this day bonding us on the deepest levels of being, levels we may or may not be aware of at this moment. Whether we are or not, the deep inner essence of us is aware, and is impressing its awareness on the dormant parts of our consciousness, awakening them as it exposes the phantom shadows generating our skewed perception of life. You could say it is washing the mortal mud off the transparent planes of our consciousness, helping us recognize the enlightened beings we truly are, and the bond we share with all creation.

Throughout every era of our self-imposed exile Love has been working behind the scenes, urging us toward unity, encouraging us to form meaningful enduring relationships that reflect the harmonious interaction we experience in the more awakened states of our being. Every day it is doing all it can to ignite a desire within us to create, maintain and preserve the beneficial, cooperative, mutually supportive, harmoniously interactive relationships capable of bringing peace to ourselves and our world. It is doing this right now.

 To the degree you and I are sensitive to Love, opening our minds and hearts to the connective tissue bonding us with our fellow humans, the barriers between ourselves and others come tumbling down, taking our fears, feelings of isolation and loneliness along with them. Degree by degree, we begin to view others as part of our human family, rather than as competitors vying with us for survival or enemies desiring to do us harm. The more our barriers tumble down, the more we recognize that every life is precious and deserving of dignity and respect, regardless of the race, creed, class or ethnicity identifying them. We naturally want all the members of our human family to live well, to not only survive, but thrive in an atmosphere where life is fair and just, where everyone has an opportunity to enjoy a healthy, productive, harmonious, fulfilling and peaceful life.

In today's intolerant chaotic divisive climate, there are times when supporting this ideal can feel like an uphill battle, especially when we find ourselves facing the resistance and hostility of those still unaware of the bond that exists between themselves and the rest of mankind. Even in the midst of these confrontations, we are fortified, for we can sense Love is with us, keeping us strong and hopeful, committed and inspired—assured that our efforts toward creating harmonious relationships that build a peaceful world are not in vain. That every inward and outward step we take toward unity and peace is having an impact, igniting a spark of recognition and remembrance within those who have forgotten who they are, and the bond they share with their fellow human beings. For a brief moment Love is subduing their fears, their confusion, their resistance and hostility. I know this, because I have witnessed Love's ability to melt the frozen hearts of those who have been traumatized and severely wounded, as well as those consumed with anger, resentment, prejudice, hatred and the kind of mad ambition that induces them to trample on others in order to grab all the power and resources they can. I have no doubt you have had occasion to witness this as well.

So, regardless of the channel Love uses to melt the hearts of the injured and angry, whether it's through you or me or an unexpected set of circumstances, Love has the power to heal the hearts and souls of every man, woman and child on Earth. Every heart melted by Love brings mankind closer to experiencing peace on Earth. In the meantime, we can not only hold love in our own hearts, but go a step further, acknowledging the love that lives in the depth of every heart and soul, including the hearts and souls of those who seem to be the most lost, the most steeped in dark beliefs and behaviors. Like I was able to do when the head of the gang confronted me in the park, we can connect with the benign unmarred soul of those who seem to have forgotten who they are, those so caught up in the nightmare of their mortal existence they cannot envision a brighter, kinder, more fair and just world. We can claim who they are beneath the disguises they and the world have fashioned for them, loving the innocent part of them, trusting they will learn to love it too.

When facing mortal opposition, we can stand with Love, planting our feet firmly on the path that leads toward harmony and peace. We can join those who have dedicated their lives to building a more cooperative harmonious, just and peaceful world. We can understand this must be done from the topside down and the inside out, rather than the other way around—realizing that trying to reunite mortals who have shattered into different states of consciousness, is like trying to glue together shattered shards of glass; it is impossible to effectively reunite them. Those living in more heightened states of consciousness may understand the limited perspective of those living in less conscious states. But those living in those less conscious states have little or no idea what life looks like or feels like in the more conscious states of their being. Equality, unity, mercy and forgiveness simply make no sense to their survival of the fittest sense of life. From their standpoint these high moral values are not only absurd, but frustrating, repugnant, unrealistic, threatening, and undesirable. Like Humpty Dumpty in the old nursery rhyme, mortals living in these less conscious states, have had a great fall. And all the kings horses and all the king's men, cannot put them back together again. Like the kings men in the nursery rhyme, we cannot put those who have fallen into less conscious states back together again. But, thankfully, Love can. For from the vantage point of Love, or God, they never fell, never shattered, nor lost awareness of their true benign nature. Despite the mortal perception and logic testifying otherwise, every human is, on some deep level, still living under Love's mighty sphere of influence, responding to the universal laws operating on every level and dimension of their being.

Ancient wisdom and contemporary science have been unraveling the mysteries of life and the universe for multiple centuries, discovering its laws and principles, interpreting them from the standpoint of their differing disciplines. Ancient wisdom, including the wisdom found in all major religions, has interpreted these laws from the standpoint of Spirit. In contrast, contemporary science has predominately investigated the laws, systems and properties of the material universe. Though in recent times a growing number of mathematicians and theoretical physicists have found their investigations crossing into the non-visible realm of metaphysics, discovering laws that equate with the universal laws and principles known to spiritual seers and mystics throughout the ages. Needless to say, they have interpreted these laws through the language of their scientific disciplines, rather than the language of Spirit. Whether we become aware of these universal laws and principles through spiritual, metaphysical or scientific means is not important. What is important is our recognition of their existence, and the value of living by them, especially the laws and principles governing and maintaining the unity that underlies existence.

Most people are familiar with spiritual and philosophical teachings testifying to the presence, power and universality of Love. Its scientific corroboration, however, may not be as familiar. In light of this, you may enjoy finding out that in the last century a series of scientific breakthroughs occurred that substantiate the holistic nature of life and the universe. For instance, the breakthrough that led Jan C. Smuts to formulate the philosophical theory of holism, or the gestalt theory stating that the whole is greater than the sum of its parts. There was Dennis Gabor's discovery of the mathematical principle of holography, which later led to the holographic imagery used in photography and films today. His discovery was so profound, other scientists began to recognize the holographic nature of their own fields. For instance, brain surgeon and Stanford researcher, Carl Pribram's recognition that our brains are holographic, and theoretical physicist, David Bohm's recognition that led to his developing the physics of holo-movement, explored in his book: *Wholeness and the Implicate Order*. Renee Weber's book: *Dialogues with Scientists and Sages* furthered the exploration of unity and wholeness. In it she shares conversations between scientists Rupert Sheldrake,

Ilya Prigogine, Steven Hawking and David Bohm with spiritual masters: Anagarika Govinda, His Holiness the Dalai Lama of Tibet, Krishnamurti and Father Bede Griffiths. Other books on the holographic nature of the universe found their way to bookstores and our shelves as well, books such as: *The Holographic Paradigm and Other Paradoxes*, edited by Ken Wilber, *The Holographic Universe* by Michael Talbot and *The Divine Matrix*, by Gregg Braden.

If, like me, you enjoy both spiritual and scientific inquiry, and feel the need for further corroboration that wholeness and unity exist beneath the surface of our everyday perception, I encourage you to read these books, as well as similar books on the subject. I have no doubt they will convince you that unity is our natural state, and that living in accord with unity makes our lives run more smoothly.

Not surprisingly, Love and unity are the clarion call of this age—a call that must, and ultimately will be, answered. As indicated earlier, the progressions of Life, and the transformative elevating impulses within man's consciousness, have already begun to usher us into the inclusivity of Love's united field, wherein intolerance, bigotry, parochialism, authoritarianism and divisiveness have no place.

We can answer this clarion call, or attempt to hang back, refusing Love's entreaty to unify. But, sooner or later Love will have its way with us, sweeping us into its coherent interactive consciousness, awakening us to the enduring bond we have with all creation. Until that prophetic moment, until we are ready to surrender to Love, and the union we share with our fellow human beings, Love and our divine essence will continue to shake up our lives—insisting we let go of the phantom shadows controlling our antiquated beliefs and behaviors. Until we do, we will be tested to our limit, enduring situation after situation, and crisis after crisis, each situation and crisis forcing us to reevaluate and alter the nature and behaviors of our lives. Some of us will react to the pain and confusion these crises bring by digging in our heels, burying our heads and hearts in the sand, and by using every means at our disposal to subvert the equality, inclusivity, integration and cooperation Love is thrusting upon us and our way of life.

For a historical moment or two, the fury of this resistance may seem to hold back the tide of Love, and the harmony and peace destined to be humanity's future, but not for long. Global unity, cooperation, compassion, harmony and peaceful coexistence are the way of the future. Our future, if we want it to be, our present, if we are willing to emancipate ourselves from our ancient fears, rising above the personal, national and global divides keeping us at odds with others.

It is time to listen closely. Our hearts are speaking, encouraging us to be the better versions of ourselves we were created to be. Versions that are benign, loving, wise and insightful, uncompromisingly compassionate and merciful in our relations with our fellow humans. It is time to honor our hearts, fully immersing ourselves in Love's transformative power, becoming the world's peacemakers and unifiers. The time to create peace is now!

THE PEACEMAKER PLEDGE

Join the peacemakers of the world.
Take this pledge each morning before you start your day.

Today I will devote myself to creating peace within myself and the world.

I will acknowledge and express the goodness that lives in the depth of my heart.

I will count my blessings, instead of complaining about my troubles.

I will fill my heart with so much love there is no room for fear, prejudice, malice or hatred to enter.

I will stay calm and centered in the face of hostility and adversity.

I will be loving, kind, compassionate, generous and forgiving.

I will be merciful and just.

I will live without judgment, putting myself in other people's shoes, mentally walking their walk, seeing the world through their eyes.

I will be a conciliator, putting balm on troubled waters wherever I encounter them.

ABOUT THE AUTHOR

Born in Los Angeles, California during the horrors and sacrifices of World War II, Marya Brunson has long held a deep desire for men to evolve beyond the hatred, prejudice, cruelty, mad ambition and war brewing in their minds, hearts and the activities of their lives. This heartfelt desire has silently sat beneath all the activities of her personal and professional life. It led her to explore the wisdom of many faiths and philosophies, taking from each the ideas that were the most inclusive and universal. Her desire for all to benefit from the universal laws and principles she discovered during her lifelong search, led her, in 1973, to become a spiritual teacher, holding workshops and talks in Los Angeles on the laws and principles underlying life and man's being. She later moved to San Diego where she continued her work, conducting year round weekly classes, as well as giving workshops and talks in other cities throughout the United States. In 2008 it led her to write a book on man's evolving consciousness, entitled: *Consciousness, Awakening to our Divine Potential. Consciousness* was followed by two young adult allegorical fantasies: *The Light of Rigel*, in 2013 and *Awakening*, in 2017.

Photo by Kat Hennessey

PEACE